Everyman

Editor: A. C. Cawley

Table of Contents

Everyman

Editor: A. C. Cawley

Here begynneth a treatyse how the hye
Fader of heuen sendeth Dethe to
somon euery creature to come and
gyue a—counte of theyr lyues in
this worlde and is in maner
of a morall playe.

French scene

Messenger.
I pray you all gyue your audyence,
And here this mater with reuerence,
By fygure a morall playe.
The Somonynge of Eueryman called it is,
That of our lyues and endynge shewes
How transytory we be all daye.
This mater is wonders precyous;
But the entent of it is more gracyous,
And swete to bere awaye.
The story sayth: Man, in the begynnynge
Loke well, and take good heed to the endynge,
Be you neuer so gay!
Ye thynke synne in the begynnynge full swete,
Whiche in the ende causeth the soule to wepe,
Whan the body lyeth in claye.
Here shall you se how Felawshyp and Iolyte,
Bothe Strengthe Pleasure and Beaute,
Wyll fade from the as floure in Maye;
For ye shall here how our Heuen Kynge
Calleth Eueryman to a generall rekenynge.
Gyue audyence, and here what he doth saye.

Scene 2. God speketh.

God.
I perceyue, here in my maieste,
How that all creatures be to me vnkynde,

Everyman

Lyuynge without drede in worldly prosperyte.
Of ghostly syght the people be so blynde,
Drowned in synne, they know me not for theyr God.
In worldely ryches is all theyr mynde;
They fere not my ryghtwysnes, the sharpe rod.
My lawe that I shewed, whan I for them dyed,
They forget clene and shedynge of my blode rede.

I hanged bytwene two theues, it can not be denyed;
To gete them lyfe I suffred to be deed;
I heled theyr fete with thornes hurt was my heed.
I coude do no more than I dyde, truely;
And nowe I se the people do clene for—sake me.
They vse the seuen deedly synnes dampnable,
As pryde, coueytyse, wrath, and lechery
Now in the worlde be made commendable;
And thus they leue of aungelles the heuenly company.
Euery man lyueth so after his owne pleasure,
And yet of theyr lyfe they be nothynge sure.
I se the more that I them forbere
The worse they be fro yere to yere.
All that lyueth appayreth faste;
Therefore I wyll, in all the haste,
Haue a rekenynge of euery mannes persone;
For, and I leue the people thus alone
In theyr lyfe and wycked tempestes,
Veryly they will become moche worse than beestes,
For now one wolde by enuy another vp ete;
Charyte they do all clene forgete.
I hoped well that euery man
In my glory sholde make his mansyon,
And therto I had them all electe;
But now I se, lyke traytours deiecte,
They thanke me not for the pleasure that I to them ment,
Nor yet for theyr beynge that I them haue lent.
I profered the people grete multytude of mercy,

3

And fewe there be that asketh it hertly.
They be so combred with worldly ryches
That nedes on them I must do iustyce,
On euery man lyuynge without fere.
Where arte thou, Deth, thou myghty messengere?

Scene 3. Dethe.

Dethe.

Almyghty God, I am here at your wyll,
Your commaundement to fulfyll.

God.

Go thou to Eueryman
And shewe hym, in my name,
A pylgrymage he must on hym take,
Whiche he in no wyse may escape;
And that he brynge with hym a sure rekenynge
Without delay or ony taryenge.

Dethe.

Lorde, I wyll in the worlde go renne ouer–all
And cruelly out–serche both grete and small.
Euery man wyll I beset that lyueth beestly
Out of Goddes lawes, and dredeth not foly.
He that loueth rychess I wyll stryke with my darte,
His syght to blynde, and fro heuen to departe—
Excepte that almes be his good frende—
In hell for to dwell, worlde without ende.
Loo, yonder I se Eueryman walkynge.

Full lytell he thynketh on my comynge;
His mynde is on flesshely lustes and his treasure,
And grete payne it shall cause hym to endure
Before the Lorde, Heuen Kynge.
Eueryman, stande styll! Whyder arte thou goynge
Thus gayly? Hast thou thy Maker forgete?

Scene 5. Eueryman.

Eueryman.
  Why askest thou?
  Woldest thou wete?

Dethe.
  Ye, syr. I wyll shewe you:
  In grete hast I am sende to the
  Fro God out of his mageste.

Eueryman.
  What, sente to me?

Dethe.
  Ye, certaynly.
  Thoughe thou haue forgete hym here,
  He thynketh on the in the heuenly spere,
  As, or we departe, thou shalte knowe.

Eueryman.

    What desyreth God of me?

Dethe.

    That shall I shewe the:
    A rekenynge he wyll nedes haue
    Without ony lenger respyte.

Eueryman.

    To gyue a rekenynge longer layser I craue;
    This blynde mater troubleth my wytte.

Dethe.

    On the thou must take a long iourney;
    Therfore thy boke of counte with the thou brynge,
    For tourne agayne thou can not by no waye.
    And loke thou be sure of thy rekenynge,
    For before God thou shalte answere, and shewe
    Thy many badde dedes, and good but a fewe;
    How thou hast spente thy lyfe, and in what wyse,
    Before the chefe Lorde of paradyse.
    Haue ado that thou were in that waye,
    For wete thou well thou shalte make none attournay.

Eueryman.

    Full vnredy I am suche rekenynge to gyue.
    I knowe the not. What messenger arte thou?

Dethe.

    I am Dethe that no man dredeth—
    For euery man I reste — and no man spareth;

Everyman

For it is Goddes commaundement
That all to me sholde be obedyent.

Eueryman.
O Deth, thou comest whan I had the leest in mynde!
In thy power it lyeth me to saue;
Yet of my good wyl I gyue the, yf thou wyl be kynde —
Ye, a thousande pounde shalte thou haue —
And dyfferre this mater tyll an other daye.

Dethe.
Eueryman, it may not be by no waye.
I set not by golde, syluer, nor rychesse,
Ne by pope emperour kynge duke, ne prynces;
For, and I wolde receyue gyftes grete,
All the worlde I myght gete;
But my custome is clene contrary.
I gyue the no respyte. Come hens, and not tary!

Eueryman.
Alas, shall I haue no lenger respyte?
I may saye Deth gyueth no warnynge!
To thynke on the, it maketh my herte seke,
For all vnredy is my boke of rekenynge.
But xii. yere and I myght haue a–bydynge,
My countynge–boke I wolde make so clere
That my rekenynge I sholde not nede to fere.
Wherfore, Deth, I praye the, for Goddes mercy,
Spare me tyll I be prouyded of remedy.

Dethe.
The auayleth not to crye, wepe, and praye;

But hast the lyghtly that thou were gone that iournaye,
And preue thy frendes yf thou can.
For wete thou well the tyde abydeth no man,
And in the worlde eche lyuynge creature
For Adams synne must dye of nature.

Eueryman.

Dethe, yf I sholde this pylgrymage take,
And my rekenynge suerly make,
Shewe me, for saynt charyte,
Sholde I not come agayne shortly?

Dethe.

No, Eueryman; and thou be ones there,
Thou mayst neuer more come here,
Trust me veryly.

Eueryman.

O gracyous God in the hye sete celestyall,
Haue mercy on me in this moost nede!
Shall I haue no company fro this vale terestryall
Of myne acqueyntaunce, that way me to lede?

Dethe.

Ye, yf ony be so hardy
That wolde go with the and bere the company.
Hye the that thou were gone to Goddes magnyfycence,
Thy rekenynge to gyue before his presence.
What, wenest thou thy lyue is gyuen the,
And thy worldely gooddes also?

Eueryman.

I had wende so, veryle.

Dethe.

Nay, nay, it was but lende the;
For as soone as thou arte go,
Another a whyle shall haue it, and than go ther–fro,
Euen as thou hast done.
Eueryman, thou arte made! Thou hast thy wyttes fyue,
And here on erthe wyll not amende thy lyue;
For sodeynly I do come.

Eueryman.

O wretched caytyfe, wheder shall I flee,
That I myght scape this endles sorowe?
Now, gentyll Deth, spare me tyll to–morowe,
That I may amende me
With good aduysement.

Dethe.

Naye, therto I wyll not consent,
Nor no man wyll I respyte;
But to the herte sodeynly I shall smyte
Without ony aduysement.
And now out of thy syght I wyll me hy.
Se thou make the redy shortely,
For thou mayst saye this is the daye
That no man lyuynge may scape a–way.

Eueryman.

Alas, I may well wepe with syghes depe!
Now haue I no maner of company

To help me in my iourney, and me to kepe;
And also my wrytynge is full vnredy.
How shall I do now for to exscuse me?
I wolde to God I had neuer be gete!
To my soule a full grete profyte it had be,
For now I fere paynes huge and grete.
The tyme passeth. Lorde, helpe, that all wrought!
For though I mourne, it auayleth nought.
The day passeth and is almoost ago;
I wote not well what for to do.
To whome were I best my complaynt to make?
What and I to Felawshyp therof spake,
And shewed hym of this sodeyne chaunce?
For in hym is all muyne affyaunce;
We haue in the worlde so many a daye
Be good frendes in sporte and playe.
I se hym yonder, certaynely.
I trust that he wyll bere me company;
Therfore to hym wyll I speke to ese my sorowe.
Well mette, Good Felawshyp, and good morowe! *Felawshyp speketh.*

Felawship.

Eueryman, good morowe, by this daye!
Syr, why lokest thou so pyteously?
If ony thynge be a–mysse, I praye the me saye,
That I may helpe to remedy.

Eueryman.

Ye, good Felawshyp, ye,
I am in greate ieoparde.

Felawship.

Everyman

My true frende, shewe to me your mynde.
I wyll not forsake the to my lyues ende,
In the waye of good company.

Eueryman.

That was well spoken and louyngly.

Felawshyp.

Syr, I must nedes knowe your heuynesse;
I haue pyte to se you in ony dystresse.
If ony haue you wronged, ye shall reuenged be,
Thoughe I on the grounde be slayne for the,

Though that I knowe before that I sholde dye.

Eueryman.

Veryly, Felawshyp, gramercy.

Felawship.

Tusshe! by thy thankes I set not a strawe.
Shewe me your grefe, and saye no more.

Eueryman.

If I my herte sholde to you breke,
And than you to tourne your mynde fro me
And wolde not me comforte whan ye here me speke,
Than sholde I ten tymes soryer be.

Felawship.

Syr, I saye as I wyll do in dede.

Eueryman.
Than be you a good frende at nede.
I haue founde you true here–before.

Felawship.
And so ye shall euermore;
For, in fayth, and thou go to hell,
I wyll not forsake the by the waye.

Eueryman.
Ye speke lyke a good frende; I byleue you well
I shall deserue it, and I maye.

Felawship.
I speke of no deseruynge, by this daye!
For he that wyll saye, and nothynge do,
Is not worthy with good company to go;
Therfore shewe me the grefe of your mynde,
As to your frende moost louynge and kynde.

Eueryman.
I shall shewe you how it is:
Commaunded I am to go a iournaye,
A longe waye harde and daungerous,
And gyue a strayte counte, without delaye,
Before the hye Iuge, Adonay.
Wherfore, I pray you, bere me company,
As ye haue promysed, in this iournaye.

Everyman

Felawship.

That is mater in dede! Promyse is duty;
But, and I sholde take suche a vyage on me,
I knowe it well, it sholde be to my payne;
Also it maketh me aferde, certayne.
But let vs take counsell here as well as we can,
For your wordes wolde fere a stronge man.

Eueryman.

Why, ye sayd yf I had nede
Ye wolde me neuer forsake, quycke ne deed,
Thoughe it were to hell, truely.

Felawship.

So I sayd, certaynely,
But suche pleasures be set a–syde, the sothe to saye;
And also, yf we toke suche a iournaye,
Whan sholde we agayne come?

Eueryman.

Naye, neuer agayne tyll the daye of dome.

Felawship.

In fayth, than wyll not I come there!
Who hath you these tydynges brought?

Eueryman.

In dede, Deth was with me here.

Felawshyp.

    Now, by God that all hathe bought,
    If Deth were the messenger,
    For no man that is lyuynge to–daye
    I wyll not go that lothe iournaye —
    Not for the fader that bygate me!

Eueryman.

    Ye promysed other wyse, parde.

Felawship.

    I wote well I sayd so, truely;
    And yet, yf thou wylte ete & drynke & make good chere,
    Or haunt to women the lusty company,
    I wolde not forsake you whyle the daye is clere,
    Trust me veryly.

Eueryman.

    Ye, therto ye wolde be redy!
    To go to myrthe, solas, and playe
    Your mynde wyll soner apply,
    Than to bere me company in my longe iournaye.

Felawship.

    Now, in good fayth, I wyll not that waye;
    But and thou wyll murder, or ony man kyll,
    In that I wyll helpe the with a good wyll.

Eueryman.

    O, that is a symple aduyse in dede.

Everyman

Gentyll felawe, helpe me in my necessyte!
We haue loued longe, and now I nede;
And now, gentyll Felawshyp, remembre me.

Felawship.
Wheder ye haue loued me or no,
By Saynt Iohan I wyll not with the go!

Eueryman.
Yet, I pray the, take the labour & do so moche for me
To brynge me forwarde, for saynt charyte,
And comforte me tyll I come without the towne.

Felawship.
Nay, and thou wolde gyue me a newe gowne,
I wyll not a fote with the go;
But, and thou had taryed, I wolde not haue lefte the so.
And as now God spede the in thy iournaye,
For from the I wyll departe as fast as I maye.

Eueryman.
Wheder a−waye, Felawshyp? Wyll thou forsake me?

Felawship.
Ye, by my faye! To God I be−take the.

Eueryman.
Farewell, good Felawshyp! For the my herte is sore.
A−dewe for euer! I shall se the no more.

Felawship.

In fayth, Eueryman, fare well now at the endynge!
For you I wyll remembre that partynge is mournynge.

Eueryman.

A−lacke, shall wee thus departe in ded —
A, Lady, helpe! — without ony more comforte?
Lo, Felawshyp forsaketh me in my moost nede.
For helpe in this worlde wheder shall I resorte?
Felawshyp here−before with me wolde mery make,
And now lytell sorowe for me dooth he take.
It is sayd, 'In prosperyte men frendes may fynde,
Whiche in aduersyte be full vnkynde.'
Now wheder for socoure shall I flee,
Syth that Felawshyp hath forsaken me?
To my kynnesmen I wyll, truely,
Prayenge them to helpe me in my necessyte.
I byleue that they wyll do so,
For kynde wyll crepe where it may not go.
I wyll go saye, for yonder I se them.
Where be ye now, my frendes and kynnesmen?

Scene 6

Kynrede.

Here be we now at your commaundement.
Cosyn, I praye you shewe vs your entent
In ony wyse, and not spare.

16

Everyman

Cosyn.
Ye, Eueryman, and to vs declare
If ye be dysposed to go ony–whyder;
For, wete you well, we wyll lyue and dye to–gyder.

Kynrede.
In welth and wo we wyll with you holde,
For ouer his kynne a man may be bolde.

Eueryman.
Gramercy, my frendes and kynnesmen kynde.
Now shall I shewe you the grefe of my mynde:
I was commaunded by a messenger,
That is a hye kynges chefe offycer.
He bad me go a pylgrymage, to my payne,
And I knowe well I shall neuer come agayne.
Also I must gyue a rekenynge strayte,
For I haue a grete enemy that hath me in wayte,
Whiche entendeth me for to hynder.

Kynrede.
What a–counte is that whiche ye must render?
That wolde I knowe.

Eueryman.
Of all my workes I must shewe
How I haue lyued and my dayes spent;
Also of yll dedes that I haue vsed
In my tyme, syth lyfe was me lent;
And of all vertues that I haue refused.
Therfore, I praye you, go thyder with me
To helpe to make myn accounte, for saynt charyte.

Everyman

Cosyn.
  What, to go thyder? Is that the mater?
  Nay, Eueryman, I had leuer fast brede and water
  All this fyue yere and more.

Eueryman.
  Alas, that euer I was bore!
  For now shall I neuer be mery,
  If that you forsake me.

Kynrede.
  A, syr, what ye be a mery man!
  Take good herte to you, and make no mone.
  But one thynge I warne you, by Saynt Anne —
  As for me, ye shall go alone.

Eueryman.
  My Cosyn, wyll you not with me go?

Cosyn.
  No, by our Lady! I haue the crampe in my to.
  Trust not to me; for, so God me spede,
  I wyll deceyue you in your moost nede.

Kynrede.
  It auayleth not vs to tyse.
  Ye shall haue my mayde with all my herte;

She loueth to go to feestes, there to be nyse,
And to daunce, and a–brode to sterte.
I wyll gyue her leue to helpe you in that iourney,
If that you and she may a–gree.

Eueryman.
Now shewe me the very effecte of your mynde:
Wyll you go with me, or abyde be–hynde?

Kynrede.
Abyde behynde? Ye, that wyll I, and I maye!
Therfore farewell tyll another daye.

Eueryman.
Howe sholde I be mery or gladde?
For fayre promyses men to me make,
But whan I haue moost nede they me forsake.
I am deceyued; that maketh me sadde.

Cosyn.
Cosyn Eueryman, farewell now,
For veryly I wyll not go with you.
Also of myne owne an vnredy rekenynge
I haue to accounte; therfore I make taryenge.
Now God kepe the, for now I go.

Scene 7

Eueryman.

A, Iesus, is all come here–to?
Lo, fayre wordes maketh fooles fayne;
They promyse, and nothynge wyll do, certayne.
My kynnesmen promysed me faythfully
For to a–byde with me stedfastly,
And now fast a–waye do they flee.
Euen so Felawshyp promysed me.
What frende were best me of to prouyde?
I lose my tyme here longer to abyde.
Yet in my mynde a thynge there is:
All my lyfe I haue loued ryches;
If that my Good now helpe my myght,
He wolde make my herte full lyght.
I wyll speke to hym in this dystresse.
Where arte thou, my Gooddes and ryches?

Scene 8

Goodes.
Who calleth me? Eueryman? What, hast thou haste?
I lye here in corners, trussed and pyled so hye,
And in chestes I am locked so fast,
Also sacked in bagges. Thou mayst se with thyn eye
I can not styre; in packes, lowe I lye.
What wolde ye haue? Lyghtly me saye.

Eueryman.
Come hyder, Good, in al the hast thou may,
For of counseyll I must desyre the.

Goodes.

Everyman

Syre, & ye in the worlde haue sorowe or aduersyte,
That can I helpe you to remedy shortly.

Eueryman.
It is another dysease that greueth me;
In this worlde it is not, I tell the so.
I am sent for, an other way to go,
To gyue a strayte counte generall
Before the hyest Iupyter of all.
And all my lyfe I haue had ioye & pleasure in the,
Therfore, I pray the, go with me;
For parauenture, thou mayst before God Almyghty
My rekenynge helpe to clene and puryfye,

For it is sayd euer amonge
That 'money maketh all ryght that is wronge.'

Goodes.
Nay, Eueryman, I synge an other songe.
I folowe no man in suche vyages;
For, and I wente with the,
Thou sholdest fare moche the worse for me.
For bycause on me thou dyd set thy mynde,
Thy rekenynge I haue made blotted and blynde,
That thyne accounte thou can not make truly —
And that hast thou for the loue of me!

Eueryman.
That wolde greue me full sore,
Whan I sholde come to that ferefull answere.
Vp, let vs go thyder to–gyder.

Goodes.

Nay, not so! I am to brytell, I may not endure.
I wyll folowe no man one fote, be ye sure.

Eueryman.

Alas, I haue the loued, and had grete pleasure
All my lyfe–dayes on good and treasure.

Goodes.

That is to thy dampnacyon, without lesynge,
For my loue is contrary to the loue euerlastynge.
But yf thou had me loued moderately durynge,
As to the poore gyue parte of me,
Than sholdest thou not in this dolour be,
Nor in this grete sorowe and care.

Eueryman.

Lo, now was I deceyued or I was ware;
And all I may wyte my spendynge of tyme.

Goodes.

What, wenest thou that I am thyne?

Eueryman.

I had went so.

Goodes.

Naye, Eueryman, I saye no.
As for a whyle I was lente the;

Everyman

A season thou hast had me in prosperyte.
My condycyon is mannes soule to kyll;
If I saue one, a thousande I do spyll.
Wenest thou that I wyll folowe the?
Nay, fro this worlde not, veryle.

Eueryman.

I had wende otherwyse.

Goodes.

Therfore to thy soule Good is a thefe;
For whan thou arte deed, this is my gyse —
Another to deceyue in this same wyse
As I haue done the, and all to his soules reprefe.

Eueryman.

O false Good, cursed thou be,
Thou traytour to God, that hast deceyued me
And caught me in thy snare!

Goodes.

Mary, thou brought thy selfe in care,
Wherof I am gladde.
I must nedes laugh; I can not be sadde.

Eueryman.

A, Good, thou hast had longe my hertely loue;
I gaue the that whiche sholde be the Lordes aboue.
But wylte thou not go with me in dede?
I praye the trouth to saye.

23

Goodes.

No, so God me spede!
Therfore fare well, and haue good daye.

Scene 9

Eueryman.

O, to whome shall I make my mone
For to go with me in that heuy iournaye?
Fyrst Felawshyp sayd he wolde with me gone;
His wordes were very pleasaunt and gaye,
But afterwarde he lefte me alone.
Than spake I to my kynnesmen, all in dyspayre,
And also they gaue me wordes fayre;
They lacked no fayre spekynge,
But all forsake me in the endynge.
Than wente I to my Goodes that I loued best,
In hope to haue comforte; but there had I leest,
For my Goodes sharpely dyd me tell
That he bryngeth many in to hell.
Than of my selfe I was ashamed,
And so I am worthy to be blamed;
Thus may I well my selfe hate.
Of whome shall I now counseyll take?
I thynke that I shall neuer spede
Tyll that I go to my Good Dede.
But, alas, she is so weke
That she can nother go nor speke;
Yet wyll I venter on her now.
My Good Dedes, where be you?

Scene 10

Good Dedes.

Here I lye, colde in the grounde.
Thy synnes hath me sore bounde,
That I can not stere.

Eueryman.

O Good Dedes, I stande in fere!
I must you pray of counseyll,
For help now sholde come ryght well.

Good Dedes.

Eueryman, I haue vnderstandynge
That ye be somoned a−counte to make
Before Myssyas, of Iherusalem kynge;
And you do by me, that iournay with you wyll I take.

Eueryman.

Therfore I come to you my moone to make.
I praye you that ye wyll go with me.

Good Dedes.

I wolde full fayne, but I can not stande, veryly.

Ereryman.

Why, is there ony thynge on you fall?

Goode Dedes.

Ye, syr, I may thanke you of all.
If ye had parfytely chered me,
Your boke of counte full redy had be.
Loke, the bokes of your workes and dedes eke
Ase how they lye vnder the fete,
To your soules heuynes.

Eueryman.

Our Lorde Iesus help me!
For one letter here I can not se.

Good Dedes.

There is a blynde rekenynge in tyme of dystres.

Eueryman.

Good Dedes, I praye you helpe me in this nede,
Or elles I am for euer dampned in dede;
Therfore helpe me to make rekenynge
Before the Redemer of all thynge,
That Kynge is, and was, and euer shall.

Good Dedes.

Eueryman, I am sory of your fall,
And fayne wolde I help you, and I were able.

Eueryman.

Good Dedes, your counseyll I pray you gyue me.

Good Dedes.

That shall I do veryly.
Thoughe that on my fete I may not go,
I haue a syster that shall with you also,
Called Knowlege, whiche shall with you abyde,
To helpe you to make that dredefull rekenynge.

Scene 11

Knowlege.

Eueryman, I wyll go with the and be thy gyde,
In they moost nede to go by thy syde.

Eueryman.

In good condycyon I am now in euery thynge,
And am holy content with this good thynge,
Thanked be God my creature.

Good Dedes.

And whan she hath brought you there
Where thou shalte hele the of thy smarte,
Than go you with your rekenynge & your Good Dedes togyder,
For to make you ioyfull at herte
Before the Blessyd Trynyte.

Eueryman.

My Good Dedes, gramercy!
I am well content, certaynly,
With your wordes swete.

Knowlege.

Now go we togyder louyngly
To Confessyon, that clensynge ryuere.

Eueryman.

For ioy I wepe; I wolde we were there!
But, I pray you, gyue me cognycyon
Where dwelleth that holy man, Confessyon.

Knowlege.

In the house of saluacyon;
We shall fynde hym in that place,
That shall vs comforte, by Goddes grace.
Lo, this is Confessyon. Knele downe & aske mercy,
For he is in good conceyte with God Almyghty.

Eueryman.

O gloryous fountayne, that all vnclennes doth claryfy,
Wasshe fro me the spottes of vyce vnclene,
That on me no synne may be sene.
I come with Knowlege for my redempcyon,
Redempte with herte and full contrycyon;
For I am commaunded a pylgrymage to take,
And grete accountes before God to make.
Now I praye you, Shryfte, moder of saluacyon,
Helpe my Good Dedes for my pyteous exclamacyon.

Scene 12

Everyman

Confessyon.

  I knowe your sorowe well, Eueryman.
Bycause with Knowlege ye come to me,
I wyll you comforte as well as I can.
And a precyous iewell I wyll gyue the,
Called penaunce, voyder of aduersyte;
Therwith shall your body chastysed be,
With abstynence & perseueraunce in Goddes seruyture.
Here shall you receyue that scourge of me,
Whiche is penaunce stronge that ye must endure,
To remembre thy Sauyour was scourged for the
With sharpe scourges, and suffred it pacyently;
So must thou or thou scape that paynful pylgrymage.
Knowlege, kepe hym in this vyage,
And by that tyme Good Dedes wyll be with the.
But in ony wyse be seker of mercy,
For your tyme draweth fast; and ye wyll saued be,
Aske God mercy, and he wyll graunte truely.
Whan with the scourge of penaunce man doth hym bynde,
The oyle of forgyuenes than shall he fynde.

Eueryman.

  Thanked be God for his gracyous werke!
For now I wyll my penaunce begyn.
This hath reioysed and lyghted my herte,
Though the knottes by paynful and harde, within.

Knowlege.

  Eueryman, loke your penaunce that ye fulfyll,
What payne that euer it to you be;
And Knowlege shall gyue you counseyll at wyll
How your accounte ye shall make clerely.

Eueryman.

O eternall God O heuenly fygure,
O way of ryghtwysnes O goodly vysyon,
Whiche dyscended downe in a vyrgyn pure
Bycause he wolde euery man redeme,
Which Adam forfayted by his dysobedyence:
O blessyd God—heed, electe and hye deuyne,
Forgyue me my greuous offence!
Here I crye the mercy in this presence.
O ghostly treasure, O raunsomer and redemer,
Of all the worlde hope and conduyter,
Myrrour of ioye, foundatour of mercy,
Whiche enlumyneth heuen and erth therby,
Here my clamorous complaynt, though it late be,
Receyue my prayers vnworthy in this heuy lyfe!
Though I be a synner moost abhomynable,
Yet let my name be wryten in Moyses table.
O Mary, praye to the Maker of all thynge,
Me for to helpe at my endynge;
And saue me from the power of my enemy,
For Deth assayleth me strongly.
And, Lady, that I may by meane of thy prayer
Of your Sones glory to be partynere,
By the meanes of his passyon, I it craue;
I besech you helpe my soule to saue.
Knowlege, gyue me the scourge of penaunce;
My flesshe therwith shall gyue acqueyntaunce.
I wyll now begyn yf God gyue me grace.

Knowlege.

Eueryman, God gyue you tyme and space!
Thus I bequeth you in the handes of our Sauyour;
Now may you make your rekenynge sure.

Everyman

Eueryman.

In the name of the Holy Trynyte,
My body sore punysshed shall be:
Take this, body, for the synne of the flesshe!
Also thou delytest to go gay and fresshe,
And in the way of dampnacyon thou dyd me brynge;
Therfore suffre now strokes of punysshynge.
Now of penaunce I wyll wade the water clere,
To saue me from Purgatory, that sharpe fyre.

Goode Dedes.

I thanke God, now I can walke and go,
And am delyuered of my sykenesse and wo.
Therfore with Eueryman I wyll go, and not spare;
His good workes I wyll helpe hym to declare.

Knowlege.

Now, Eueryman, be mery and glad!
Your Good Dedes cometh now; ye may not be sad.
Now is your Good Dedes hole and sounde,
Goynge vpryght vpon the grounde.

Eueryman.

My herte is lyght, and shal be euermore;
Now wyll I smyte faster than I dyde before.

Good Dedes.

Eueryman, pylgryme, my specyall frende,
Blessyd be thou without ende!
For the is preparate the eternall glory.
Ye haue me made hole and sounde,
Therfore I wyll byde by the in euery stounde.

31

Eueryman.

Welcome, my Good Dedes! Now I here thy voyce
I wepe for very swetenes of loue.

Knowlege.

Be no more sad, but euer reioyce;
God seeth thy lyuynge in his trone aboue.
Put on this garment to thy behoue,
Whiche is wette with your teres,
Or elles before God you may it mysse,
Whan ye to your iourneys ende come shall.

Eueryman.

Gentyll Knowlege, what do ye it call?

Knowlege.

It is a garment of sorowe;
Fro payne it wyll you borowe.
Contrycyon it is
That getteth forgyuenes;
He pleaseth God passynge well.

Good Dedes.

Eueryman, wyll you were it for your hele?

Eueryman.

Now blessyde be Iesu, Maryes sone,
For now haue I on true contrycyon;
And lette vs go now without taryenge.

Good Dedes, haue we clere our rekenynge?

Good Dedes.
Ye, in dede, I haue it here.

Eueryman.
Than I trust we nede not fere.
Now, frendes, let vs not parte in twayne.

Knowlege.
Nay, Eueryman, that wyll we not, certayne.

Good Dedes.
Yet must thou lede with the
Thre persones of grete myght.

Eueryman.
Who sholde they be?

Good Dedes.
Dyscrecyon and Strength they hyght,
And thy Beaute may not abyde behynde.

Knowlege.
Also ye must call to mynde
Your Fyue Wyttes as for your counseylours.

Good Dedes.

You must haue them redy at all houres.

Eueryman.
Howe shall I gette them hyder?

Knowlege.
You must call them all togyder,
And they wyll here you in-contynent.

Eueryman.
My frendes, come hyder and be present,
Dyscrecyon, Strengthe, my Fyue Wyttes, and Beaute.

Scene 13

Beaute.
Here at your wyll we be all redy.
What wolde ye that we shold do?

Good Dedes.
That ye wolde with Eueryman go,
And help hym in his pylgrymage.
Aduyse you wyll ye with him or not in that vyage?

Strength.
We wyll brynge hym all thyder,
To his helpe and comforte ye may byleue me.

Dyscrecion.

So wyll we go with hym all togyder.

Eueryman.

Almyghty God, loued may thou be!
I gyue the laude that I haue hyder brought
Strength, Dyscrecyon, Beaute, & V. Wyttes. Lacke I nought.
And my Good Dedes, with Knowlege clere,
All be in company at my wyll here.
I desyre no more to my besynes.

Strengthe.

And I, Strength, wyll gy you stande in dystres,
Though thou wolde in batayle fyght on the grounde.

V. Wyttes.

And though it were thrugh the worlde rounde,
We wyll not departe for swete ne soure.

Beaute.

No more wyll I vnto dethes houre,
What so euer therof befall.

Dyscrecion.

Eueryman, aduyse you fyrst of all;
Go with a good aduysement and delyberacyon.
We all gyue you vertuous monycyon
That all shall be well.

Everyman

Eueryman.

My frendes, harken what I wyll tell:
I praye God rewarde you in his heuenly spere.
Now herken, all that be here,
For I wyll make my testament
Here before you all present:
In almes halfe my good I wyll gyue with my handes twayne
In the way of charyte with good entent,
And the other halfe styll shall remayne
In queth, to be retourned there it ought to be.
This I do in despyte of the fende of hell,
To go quyte out of his perell
Euer after and this daye.

Knowlege.

Eueryman, herken what I saye:
Go to Presthode, I you aduyse,
And receyue of hym in ony wyse
The holy sacrament and oyntement togyder.
Than shortly se ye tourne agayne hyder;
We wyll all abyde you here.

V. Wwyttes.

Ye, Eueryman, hye you that ye redy were.
There is no Emperour, Kynge, Duke, ne Baron,
That of God hath commycyon
As hath the leest preest in the worlde beynge;
For of the blessyd sacraments pure and benygne
He bereth the keyes, and therof hath the cure
For mannes recempcyon — it is euer sure —
Whiche God for our soules medycyne
Gaue vs out of his herte with grete pyne.
Here in this transytory lyfe, for the and me,
The blessyd sacraments vii. there be:

36

Baptym, confyrmacyon, with preesthode good,
And the sacrament of Goddes precyous flesshe & blod,
Maryage, the holy extreme vnccyon, and penaunce.
These seuen be good to haue in remembraunce,
Gracyous sacraments of hye deuynyte.

Eueryman.

Fayne wolde I receyue that holy body,
And mekely to my ghostly fader I wyll go.

V. Wyttes.

Eueryman, that is the best that ye can do.
God wyll you to saluacyon brynge,
For preesthode excedeth all other thynge:
To vs holy scrypture they do teche,
And conuerteth man fro synne, heuen to reche;
God hath to them more power gyuen
Than to ony aungell that is in heuen.
With v. wordes he may consecrate,
Goddes body in flesshe and blode to make,
And handeleth his Maker bytwene his handes.
The preest byndeth and vnbyndeth all bandes,
Bothe in erthe and in heuen.
Thou mynystres all the sacramentes seuen;
Though we kysse thy fete, thou were worthy.
Thou arte surgyon that cureth synne deedly;
No remedy we fynde vnder God
But all onely preesthode.
Eueryman, God gaue preest that dygnyte,
And setteth them in his stede amonge vs to be;
Thus be they aboue aungelles in degree.

Knowlege.

If preestes be good, it is so, suerly.
But whan Iesu hanged on the crosse with grete smarte,
There he gaue out of his blessyd herte
The seuen sacraments in grete tourment;
He solde them not to vs, that Lorde omnypotent.
Therfore Saynt Peter the apostell dothe saye
That Iesus curse hath all they
Whiche God theyr Sauyour do by or sell,
Or they for ony money do take or tell.
Synfull preestes gyueth the synners example bad:
Theyr chyldren sytteth by other mennes fyres, I haue harde;
And some haunteth womens company
With vnclene lyfe, as lustes of lechery.
These be with synne made blynde.

V. Wyttes.

I trust to God no suche may we fynde;
Therfore let vs preesthode honour,
And folowe theyr doctryne for our soules socoure.
We be theyr shepe, and they shepeherdes be
By whome we all be kepte in suerte.
Peas! For yonder I se Eueryman come,
Which hath made true satysfaccyon.

Good Dedes.

Me thyhnke it is he in ded.

Eueryman.

Now Iesu be your alder spede!
I haue receyued the sacrament for my redempycon,
And than myne extreme vnccyon.
Blessyd be all they that counseyled me to take it!
And now, frendes, let vs go with—out longer respyte.

Everyman

I thanke God that ye haue taryed so longe.
Now set eche of you on this rodde your honde,
And shortely folowe me.
I go before there I wolde be. God be our gyde!

Strength.

Eueryman, we wyll not fro you go
Tyll ye haue done this vyage longe.

Dyscrecion.

I, Dyscrecyon, wyll byde by you also.

Knowlege.

And though this pylgrymage be neuer so stronge,
I wyll neuer parte you fro.

Strength.

Eueryman, I wyll be as sure by the
As euer I dyde by Iudas Machabee.

Eueryman.

Alas, I am so faynt I may not stande;
My lymmes vnder me do folde.
Frendes, let vs not tourne agayne to this lande,
Not for all the worldes golde;
For in to this caue must I crepe
And tourne to erth, and there to slepe.

Beaute.

What, in to this graue? Alas!

Eueryman.

Ye, there shall ye consume, more and lesse.

Beaute.

And what, sholde I smoder here?

Eueryman.

Ye, by my fayth, and neuer more appere.
In this worlde lyue no more we shall,
But in heuen before the hyest Lorde of all.

Beaute.

I crosse out all this. Adewe, by Saynt Iohan!
I take my tappe in my lappe and am gone.

Eueryman.

What, Beaute, whyder wyll ye?

Beaute.

Peas! I am defe. I loke not behynde me,
Not & thou wolde gyue me all the golde in thy chest.

Scene 14

Eueryman.

    Alas, wherto may I truste?
    Beaute gothe fast awaye fro me.
    She promysed with me to lyue and dye.

Strength.

    Eueryman, I wyll the also forsake and denye;
    Thy game lyketh me not at all.

Eueryman.

    Why, than, ye wyll forsake me all?
    Swete Strength, tary a lyttel space.

Strengthe.

    Nay, syr, by the rode of grace!
    I wyll hye me from the fast,
    Though thou wepe to thy herte to–brast.

Eueryman.

    Ye wolde euer byde by me, ye sayd.

Strength.

    Ye, I haue you ferre ynoughe conueyde.
    Ye be olde ynoughe, I vnderstande,
    Your pylgrymage to take on hande.
    I repent me that I hyder came.

Eueryman.

    Strength, you to dysplease I am to blame.
    Wyll ye breke promyse that is dette?

Strength.

In fayth, I care not.
Thou arte but a foole to complayne;
You spend your speche and wast your brayne.
Go thryst the in to the grounde.

Scene 15

Everyman.

I had wende surer I sholde you haue founde.
He that trusteth in his Strength,
She hym deceyueth at the length.
Bothe Strength and Beaute forsaketh me;
Yet they promysed me fayre and louyngly.

Dyscrecion.

Eueryman, I wyll after Strength be gone.
As for me, I wyll leue you alone.

Eueryman.

Why, Dyscrecyon, wyll ye forsake me?

Dyscrecion.

Ye, in faytyh, I wyll go fro the,
For whan Strength goth before
I folowe after euer more.

Eueryman.

Yet, I pray the, for the loue of the Trynyte,
Loke in my graue ones pyteously.

Dyscrecion.

Nay, so nye wyll I not come.
Fare well, euerychone!

Scene 16

Eueryman.

O, all thynge fayleth, saue God alone —
Beaute, Strength, and Dyscrecyon;
For whan Deth bloweth his blast,
They all renne fro me full fast.

V. Wyttes.

Eueryman, my leue now of the I take.
I wyll folowe the other, for here I the forsake.

Eueryman.

Alas, than may I wayle and wepe,
For I toke you for my best frende.

V. Wyttes.

I wyll no lenger the kepe.
Now fare well, and there an ende.

Scene 17

Eueryman.

O Iesu, helpe! All hath forsaken me.

Good Dedes.

Nay, Eueryman, I wyll byde with the.
I wyll not forsake the in dede;
Thou shalte fynde me a good frende at nede.

Eueryman.

Gramercy, Good Dedes! Now may I true frendes se.
They haue forsaken me, euerychone;
I loued them better than my Good Dedes alone.
Knowlege, wyll ye forsake me also?

Knowlege.

Ye, Eueryman, whan ye to Deth shall go;

But not yet, for no maner of daunger.

Everyman.

Gramercy, Knowlege, with all my herte.

Knowlege.

Nay, yet I wyll not from hens departe
Tyll I se where ye shall be–come.

Everyman

Eueryman.

Me thynke, alas, that I must be gone
To make my rekenynge and my dettes paye,
For I se my tyme is nye spent awaye.
Take example, all ye that this do here or se,
How they that I loued best do forsake me,
Except my Good Dedes that bydeth truely.

Good Dedes.

All erthly thynges is but vanyte:
Beaute, Strength and Dyscrecyon do man forsake,
Folysshe frendes and kynnesmen that fayre spake —
All fleeth saue Good Dedes, and that am I.

Eueryman.

Haue mercy on me, God moost myghty,
And stande by me, thou moder & mayde, Holy Mary!

Good Dedes.

Fere not; I wyll speke for the.

Eueryman.

Here I crye God mercy.

Good Dedes.

Shorte our ende and mynysshe our payne;
Let vs go and neuer come agayne.

Eueryman.

In to thy handes, Lorde, my soule I commende;
Receyue it, Lorde, that it be not lost.
As thou me boughtest, so me defende,
And saue me from the fendes boost,
That I may appere with that blessyd hoost
That shall be saued at the day of dome.
In manus tuas , of myghtes moost
For euer, *Commendo spiritum meum.*

Knowlege.

Now hath he suffred that we all shall endure;
The Good Dedes shall make all sure.
Now hath he made endynge;
Me thynketh that I here aungelles synge
And make grete ioy and melody
Where Euerymannes soule receyued shall be.

Scene 18

The Aungell.

Come, excellente electe spouse, to Iesu!
Here aboue thou shalte go
Bycause of thy synguler vertue.
Now thy soule is taken thy body fro,
Thy rekenynge is crystall–clere.
Now shalte thou in to the heuenly spere,
Vnto the whiche all ye shall come
That lyueth well before the daye of dome.

Scene 19

Doctour.
This morall men may haue in mynde.
Ye herers, take it of worth, olde and yonge,
And forsake Pryde, for he deceyueth you in the ende;
And remembre Beaute, V. Wyttes, Strength, & Dyscrecyon,
They all at the last do Eueryman forsake,
Saue his Good Dedes there dothe he take.
But be–ware, for and they be small,
Before God he hath no helpe at all:
None excuse may be there for Eueryman.
Alas, how shall he do than?
For after dethe amendes may no man make,
For than mercy and pyte doth hym forsake.
If his rekenynge be not clere whan he doth come,
God wyll saye, *'Ite, maledicti, in ignem eternum.'*
And he that hath his accounte hole and sounde,
Hye in heuen he shall be crounde.
Vnto which place God brynge vs all thyder,
That we may lyue body and soule togyder.
Therto helpe the Trynyte!
Amen, saye ye, for saynt charyte.
FINIS.

Thus endeth this morall playe of Eueryman.
Imprynted at London in Poules
chyrche yarde by me
Iohan Skot.

47